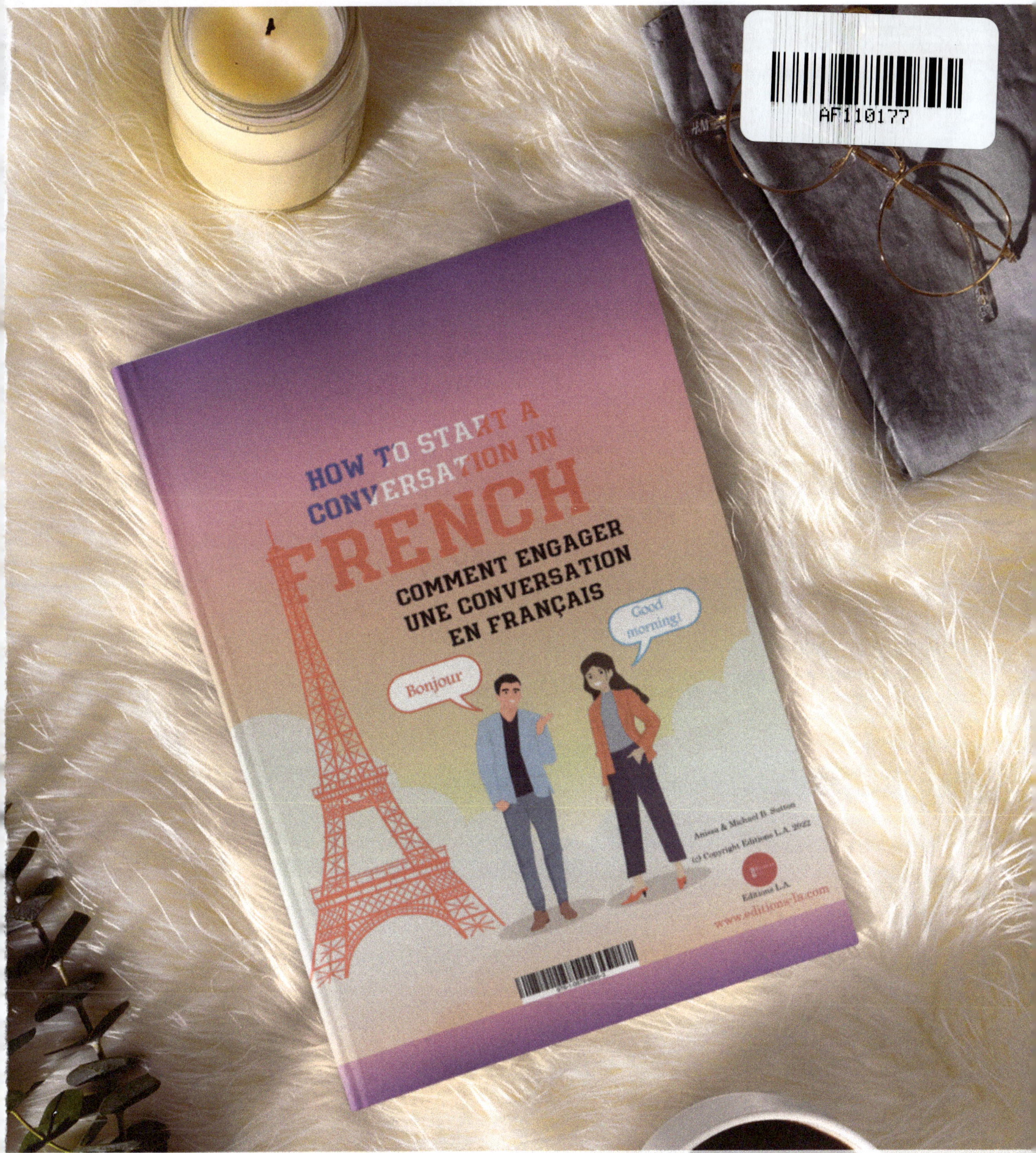
HOW TO START A CONVERSATION IN
FRENCH
COMMENT ENGAGER UNE CONVERSATION EN FRANÇAIS
Bonjour
Good morning!
Anissa & Michael D. Sutton
(c) Copyright Editions L.A. 2022
Editions L.A.
www.editions-la.com

Pump it up Magazine

TABLE OF CONTENTS

Letter from The Editor — 5
Anissa Sutton

FITNESS — 12
- 10 Essential Self-Defense Tips
- 4 Weeks Workout Plan

BEAUTY — 21
Homemade Recipes for a Gorgeous Skin

QUIZZ — 28
How Anxious Are You?

COVER STORY
JULIANA "KILLER" MILLER
🌟 Interview with UFC and MMA Champion Empowering Women and Kids Against Bullying & Abuse

HAPPY HOLIDAYS!
- Best Holiday Gift Ideas
- Must-Watch Christmas Movies
- Our Favorite Christmas Songs

WELLNESS
- How to Say NO!
- Heal with Binaural Beats & Frequencies
- How Do Crosswords Help Your Brain?
- How to Handle the Haters

HUMANITARIAN AWARENESS
How to Make the World a Better Place by Helping Others

Reach for the Stars - While Standing on Earth!

Pump it up MAGAZINE ®

PUMP IT UP MAGAZINE
LINKS

WEBSITE
www.pumpitupmagazine.com

FACEBOOK
www.facebook.com/pumpitupmagazine

TWITTER
www.twitter.com/pumpitupmag

SOUNDCLOUD
www.soundcloud.com/pumpitupmagazine

INSTAGRAM
pumpitupmagazine

PINTEREST
www.pinterest.com/pumpitupmagazine

PUMP IT UP MAGAZINE
30721 Russell Ranch Road
Suite 140
Westlake Village,
California 91362
United States

 (818)514 – 0038(Ext:102)
 info@pumpitupmagazine.com

Letter from the Editor

Hey there, Fabulous Readers,

You might be wondering,
"How did MMA & UFC Champion Juliana 'Killer' Miller end up on our cover?"
Well, let me spill the beans!

Thanks to a delightful twist of fate and the allure of our August edition, I had the pleasure of being introduced to Juliana by none other than Grandmixer GMS. Not only is Grandmixer GMS an esteemed DJ at KPIU Radio, the official station of Pump It Up Magazine, but he also graced our August cover – a true gem in our network!

Get ready for a whirlwind of excitement in this special December edition!

From beauty recipes for that perfect glow to brain-boosting crossword tips, energizing fitness tips, handling haters like a pro, exploring the healing power of binaural beats and frequencies, and yes, self-defense tips – we've packed this issue to make December absolutely amazing.

But wait, there's more! Get into the holiday spirit with our ultimate guide to the best gifts, must-watch Christmas movies and heartwarming tunes that'll create magical moments around your Christmas tree.

And let's not forget our focus on making the world a better place through humanitarian awareness.

Remember, Pump It Up Magazine isn't just a name; it's a philosophy. It's about infusing hope, strength, and life into every page, making dreams reality, and uplifting lives while reminding you to reach for the stars while standing on earth. It's a call to dream big, stay grounded, and embrace the magic of possibility every step of the way.

Wishing you a joyful holiday season filled with warmth, laughter, and cherished moments with loved ones as you flip through these awesome pages!

Anissa Sutton

CONTRIBUTORS

FOUNDER & EDITOR IN CHIEF
Anissa Sutton

EDITOR
Michael B. Sutton

MARKETING
Grace Rose

PARTNERS

Editions L.A.
www.editions-la.com

The Sound Of L.A.
www.thesoundofla.com

Info Music
www.infomusic.fr

YMC
yourmusicconsultant.com

Photo credits
Juan Cardenas
@desautomatas
Juliana Miller

Rick Little
GMS
Lisa Holtz
Manolo Hernandez

Juliana "Killer" Miller

Photo credits
Juan Cardenas @desautomatas

**Unstoppable Fearless Strength:
Where Triumph Begins!**

In the world of UFC and Mixed Martial Arts (MMA), Juliana "Killer" Miller isn't just a skilled fighter—she embodies resilience, empowerment, and takes a firm stand against bullying and abuse. Born on May 7, 1996, in San Diego, California, this 5'7" fighter has made her mark in the Flyweight division, representing both Team Hurricane Awesome and Sikjitsu after moving her training base from San Diego to Spokane, Washington.

Early Journey and Noteworthy Achievements

Juliana's foray into combat sports began with her quest for self-defense through Brazilian jiu-jitsu. Her amateur career boasted an impressive undefeated streak of 6-0, showcasing her evolving skills and unwavering determination. Progressing to the professional circuit, *she claimed victories in renowned events like California Cage Wars 13 and Invicta FC, solidifying her position as a force to be reckoned with in the MMA scene.*

However, *her defining moment unfolded during Season 30 of "The Ultimate Fighter" (TUF), a prestigious event televised on ESPN+.* Juliana's journey in this competition underscored her exceptional abilities and unwavering perseverance. It culminated in a resounding triumph during the high-stakes final match at the UFC Apex facility on **August 6, 2022, crowning her as the champion of TUF Season 30—a pivotal milestone in her illustrious career.**

The nickname "Killer" was given to her by her MMA coach Manolo Hernandez!

Why Opponents Should Fear Her

Juliana strikes fear into her opponents with her unmatched skill, unwavering determination, and an impressive track record. From an undefeated amateur career to triumphs in events like California Cage Wars 13 and Invicta FC, she's dominated the cage. Her TUF Season 30 success cements her reputation as a fierce competitor, showcasing unmatched skill, focus, and determination in every fight.

Advocacy Against Bullying and Abuse: A Personal Crusade

Juliana's crusade against bullying and abuse is deeply rooted in her personal experiences. She vocalizes her journey, stating:

*"My drive to fight comes from my past.
I aim to prove that overcoming adversities is achievable!"*

Her commitment extends far beyond the confines of the ring. Juliana is dedicated to empowering vulnerable individuals, particularly women and children, against the dangers of bullying and abuse. Her resilience isn't confined to the octagon; it's reflected in her commitment to tackling societal challenges by advocating mental wellness and self-empowerment.

Juliana "Killer" Miller

1. HOW DID YOUR MMA JOURNEY BEGIN AND HOW HAS IT IMPACTED YOUR MENTAL RESILIENCE AND WELL-BEING?

My MMA journey began when I was younger; I didn't defend myself and ended up in a precarious situation. I then vowed to never let anyone touch me again. My friends encouraged me to buy a gun, but it's impractical to rely solely upon a gun, especially in settings influenced by alcohol and substances. And in many places, you cannot even bring a firearm. That's why I decided to focus on self-defense – specifically for women – and Jiu-Jitsu is perfect for that. Two years of intensive training ensued, marked by numerous competitions – where I was killing it – and that instilled confidence in me and my abilities.

*So I asked my coach, Manolo Hernandez, if I could teach a women's self-defense class, and he said "f*** no, the only fight you were ever in you got 'effed up."*

Undeterred, I asked what it would take to instruct the course. His response: win three amateur MMA fights. I looked at him and I said, "Yes, sir." And I did just that! *I won my first three amateur fights, two of them in under a minute, and I even broke an opponent's arm. I was then able to teach my women's self-defense course! Ilima-Lei Macfarlane helped me, and about 45 women showed up. We hosted it at 10th Planet San Diego, and it was an incredible experience.*

Simultaneously, my MMA matches became an outlet to release pent-up energy, offering a legal avenue to punch someone and not get into trouble. And considering everything I had been through, MMA etched a transformative chapter in my life and impacted my mental resilience and well-being because it gave me something positive to focus on while, at the same time, releasing my life troubles. This allowed me to work on my mental health by being physically active, while also helping other people through the women's self-defense course. That really helped me because women – specifically those who have been through traumatic situations – often change their life where they stop going out and stop having fun, but I wanted the opposite: I wanted to learn how to feel confident in my daily life and activities, rather than being fearful, which is what happens to many people.

2. WHAT KEY INSIGHTS OR LESSONS DID YOU GAIN FROM THE ULTIMATE FIGHTER, ESPECIALLY REGARDING MENTAL STRENGTH AND SELF-DISCOVERY?

When I got the call about doing The Ultimate Fighter, I had just lost to Claire Guthrie at Invicta FC 44, so I didn't think that I was a good fighter. *I was actually preparing to join the Air Force. However when I got the message that they really wanted me to be on the Ultimate Fighter, in my head I had an, "eff it, this is my last opportunity" mentality. So from the second I got into quarantine. I flipped the script: I ran hard every day and while running I'd tell myself, "You're the best, you're the Ultimate Fighter Champion," and I ingrained that into my soul.* That's the only thing I let myself think, especially when I would have severe doubts. And as I got into the TUF house I did the same thing. Although I was scared, my mentality was, "this is probably the last time I'm going to fight, so I'm going to go out as if it were my last fight and show the world who I am." That was my mindset going into the fights, and while others were partying or hanging out with everyone, I locked myself in my room and would meditate, do yoga, and read quotes from my emotional intelligence courses. I was very reclusive and I didn't want friends or to talk to people. All I wanted was to win and I knew what I had to do: take care of my weight and train hard, and then whatever was going to happen would happen.

That showed me what focus can do because pre-Ultimate Fighter, I was working four jobs: I worked at a cryotherapy facility; I was a personal assistant for a girl named Sarah that worked in cancer hospital; I puppy-sat on the weekends for Coach Bill, Ilima-Lei Macfarlane and Sarah; and I worked at American Icon Photographs, so I never had time to just focus on training because I lived in San Diego and to pay bills and was trying to save money, so I was never able to focus solely on training, but while I was on TUF I was able to focus like never before. That was an incredible experience that I wouldn't change for the world.

3. BESIDES MMA ACHIEVEMENTS, WHAT DRIVES YOUR ASPIRATIONS, ESPECIALLY IN MENTAL HEALTH ADVOCACY OR PERSONAL DEVELOPMENT?

Trying to be the best possible version of myself every day. Once you struggle with mental health issues, they don't go away – they can either get better or worse, depending on you. *Your brain is a muscle that you have to keep working daily in order to keep it strong. I had surgery on my left arm and haven't been using it for 2 months, so it's weak compared to my right arm. Thus, you have to use your brain muscle every day.* **I highly suggest getting involved in emotional intelligence courses!** I'll preach that forever, and it's something I want to re-enroll in. As much as I'd like to say I learned my lesson and I'm a healed, perfect person, I still battle these mental health issues daily, and for me to be the best version of myself, I have to work this brain muscle constantly. The best way to do it is meditation, reading, writing, scribing – always working that brain muscle.

4. REFLECTING ON YOUR MMA SUCCESS, HOW DO YOU USE YOUR ACHIEVEMENTS, LIKE WINNING THE ULTIMATE FIGHTER, TO INSPIRE OTHERS IN PURSUING THEIR GOALS?

To be honest, I don't feel like I've had the most MMA success yet. However, winning The Ultimate Fighter definitely gives me the confidence to say if I can do it, you can too. The thing I preached most on The Ultimate Fighter was that anything is possible and I truly believe that. *Anything is possible and that's something that I would love to instill into the next generation.*

Something is not possible if you don't believe that it is; you have to believe it and you can achieve it, BUT, it takes a lot of work for you to really be able to believe this and to do it. So, work on that brain muscle.

5. HOW WILL YOU FURTHER AID WOMEN AND CHILDREN AFFECTED BY ABUSE OR ASSAULT, FOSTERING A SAFER ENVIRONMENT WITHIN AND BEYOND COMBAT SPORTS?

I plan on using my voice and the platform I've created to do positive outreach. Pre-COVID I held women's self-defense courses at the YMCA, and I plan to continue holding such courses. *In the near-future I will create online self-defense courses, and I will continue to preach to the world about the importance of self-defense for youth, because children are the most targeted, as they are the most vulnerable and the easiest to attack. I will always wholeheartedly preach to everyone about getting your children into self-defense, MMA, and specifically, Jiu-Jitsu classes.*

I believe the most important step for creating a safer environment for women and children is getting them involved in self-defense. A gun at home isn't going to save you from a bad situation, but self-awareness will. Not only do these classes create self-awareness, but they work your brain muscle, they create confidence, and they teach you the specific moves necessary for each situation.

For example, if someone is grabbing your throat, you'll know how to defend yourself. *And defense isn't about beating someone up; it's about removing yourself from the situation, such as getting their hands off you so you can get away to safety.* And I think that is most important.

6. LOOKING AHEAD, HOW WOULD YOU LIKE TO BE REMEMBERED FOR YOUR CONTRIBUTIONS TO MENTAL HEALTH AWARENESS AND THE MMA WORLD?

I'm not sure how I want to be remembered. I feel I have quite a path ahead of me of things I would like to accomplish, but if there is one human out there, who my voice could have helped or inspired, then that is enough for me. I do want to be remembered as a champion, as a person who helped change the world to make it a better place, but I don't feel I have fulfilled those tasks yet. I have quite a bit of work to do before I feel like I deserve to be remembered and acknowledged as somebody incredible and great so, I'd better get back to work.

Editions L.A.

DIGITAL CREATIVE AGENCY

We Transform Your Vision Into Creative Results

Editions L.A. is a full-service agency based in Los Angeles. Our company is a collective of amazing people striving to build delightful services
We believe that is all about getting your message across clearly and with a "Wow!" thrown in for good measure.

Our Awesome Services

Branding

We build, style and tone your brand identity from the ground up.
We rebrand established bands, brands or businesses.

Merchandise Store
Website design and E-Commerce
Website updates

Digital Marketing

CD Cover | Banners | Logo design | Flyers | Brochures | Leaflets | Print ads | Magazine covers & artworks
Facebook / twitter / instagram / youtube artworks
| Book cover
Infographics | Icon Design |
| TshirtsProduct Labels | Presentation slides
Corporate graphics
Professional photo editing & enhancing
Redesign existing elements
YouTube Optimization and Monetization
Youtube Video Editing
Lyric Video and Advertising Design.

Publishing

BOOK COVER DESIGN
EBOOK FORMATTING SERVICES
and distribution on major platforms
(Amazon, Barnes & Nobles..)

Tell us about your dream and we will make it true!

Editions L.A.
7210 Jordan Avenue Suite B42, Canoga Park, California 91303, United States
info@edtions-la.com
Website: www.editions-la.com

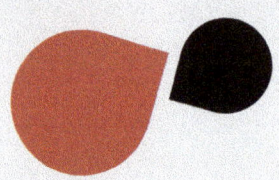

10 Essential Self-Defense Tips: Your Ultimate Guide to Personal Safety!

In an ever-changing world, knowing how to defend oneself is crucial for personal safety. Whether you're walking alone, commuting, or merely going about your daily routine, being prepared can make a significant difference. Here are ten essential self-defense tips that can empower you to protect yourself in challenging situations.

1. STAY AWARE OF YOUR SURROUNDINGS:
Awareness is key. Stay alert and observant of your surroundings. Knowing what's happening around you allows you to identify potential threats and act accordingly.

2. TRUST YOUR INSTINCTS:
If something feels off or makes you uncomfortable, trust your instincts. Often, your gut feeling can signal potential danger. Don't ignore it.

3. MAINTAIN CONFIDENT BODY LANGUAGE:
Show confidence in your posture and demeanor. Walk tall, make eye contact, and keep your head up. Predators tend to target individuals who appear vulnerable or unsure.

4. PRACTICE VERBAL ASSERTIVENESS:
Use a firm and assertive voice when setting boundaries or saying no. Your tone can deter potential attackers and signal that you're not an easy target.

5. LEARN BASIC SELF-DEFENSE MOVES:
Enroll in a self-defense class or learn basic techniques online. Simple moves like palm strikes, knee jabs, or elbow strikes can be effective in defending yourself.

6. CARRY PERSONAL SAFETY DEVICES:
Consider carrying items like pepper spray, a personal alarm, or a whistle. These tools can help attract attention or provide a means to defend yourself if necessary."

7. CREATE DISTANCE:
If confronted, create space between you and the threat. Use verbal commands to maintain distance and buy time to escape or seek help.

8. ESCAPE ROUTES AND SAFE HAVENS:
Always be aware of nearby exits or safe places you can quickly access. Plan escape routes in unfamiliar locations for added preparedness.

9. AVOID RISKY SITUATIONS:
Trust your judgment and avoid potentially risky situations, especially at night or in poorly lit areas. Opt for well-lit paths and populated areas whenever possible.

10. PRACTICE REGULARLY:
Self-defense is a skill that improves with practice. Regularly revisit your self-defense techniques to reinforce your skills and build confidence.

For more helpful tips, visit www.pumpitupmagazine.com/
Remember, while these tips can enhance your safety, the goal is always to evade danger whenever possible. Prioritize your well-being and take proactive steps to protect yourself. Stay vigilant, stay prepared, and prioritize your safety above all else., For further guidance and expert advice on self-defense techniques, consider seeking instruction from a professional self-defense instructor or martial arts expert in your area. Stay safe and empowered!

4 WEEKS WORKOUT PLAN

SUN
- 45 jumping jacks
- 15 squats
- 5 jump squats
- 50 Russian twists
- 30 second plank
- 10 standing calf raises
- 5 kneeling pushups
- 30 seconds Superman
- 10 lunges (each leg)
- 40 crunches

MON
- 45 jumping jacks
- 15 squats
- 5 jump squats
- 50 Russian twists
- 30 second plank
- 10 standing calf raises
- 5 kneeling pushups
- 30 seconds Superman
- 10 lunges (each leg)
- 40 crunches

TUES
- 45 jumping jacks
- 15 squats
- 5 jump squats
- 50 Russian twists
- 30 second plank
- 10 standing calf raises
- 5 kneeling pushups
- 30 seconds Superman
- 10 lunges (each leg)
- 40 crunches

WED
- 45 jumping jacks
- 15 squats
- 5 jump squats
- 50 Russian twists
- 30 second plank
- 10 standing calf raises
- 5 kneeling pushups
- 30 seconds Superman
- 10 lunges (each leg)
- 40 crunches

THURS
- 45 jumping jacks
- 15 squats
- 5 jump squats
- 50 Russian twists
- 30 second plank
- 10 standing calf raises
- 5 kneeling pushups
- 30 seconds Superman
- 10 lunges (each leg)
- 40 crunches

FRI
- 45 jumping jacks
- 15 squats
- 5 jump squats
- 50 Russian twists
- 30 second plank
- 10 standing calf raises
- 5 kneeling pushups
- 30 seconds Superman
- 10 lunges (each leg)
- 40 crunches

SAT
- 45 jumping jacks
- 15 squats
- 5 jump squats
- 50 Russian twists
- 30 second plank
- 10 standing calf raises
- 5 kneeling pushups
- 30 seconds Superman
- 10 lunges (each leg)
- 40 crunches

MUST WATCH

CHRISTMAS

MOVIES

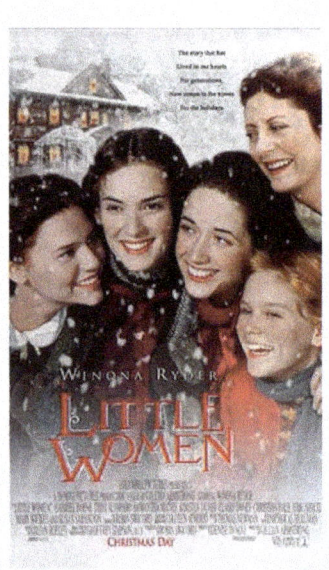

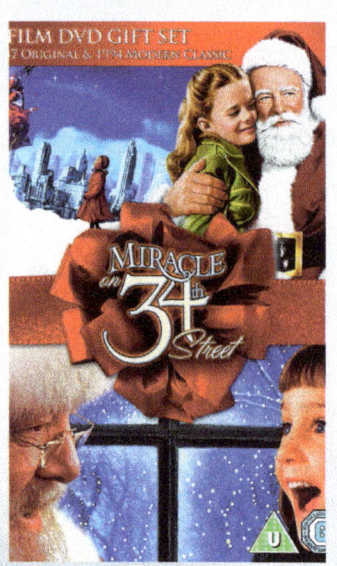

Pump it up
magazine

Reach for the stars,
while standing on earth!

HAPPY HOLIDAYS!
CHRISTMAS SONGS

This selection is sure to fill your heart with the joy of Christmas!

WWW.PUMPITUPMAGAZINE.COM/RADIO

GRANDMIXER GMS

Drops Fire Beats:
Where Hip-Hop meets Soulful Vibes
feat.

DJ NASTY-NES | RICH TYCOON

GrandMixer GMS (feat. Nasty Nes)
Nasty Nes Calling From Los Angeles

Rich Tycoon x GrandMixer GMS
Everybody Wanna Ride (When They C U Rollin') (Freestyle) (Clean)

I Need A Bang'er
GrandMixer GMS

Get ready to feel that heat and move to those sick beats!

Spotligt

@GRANDMIXERGMS

www.pumpitupmagazine.com

YOUR MUSIC CONSULTANT

"YOU BELIEVE, SO DO WE!"

We Can Help You To Grow Your Business

We are a monthly based service, we put faith in artists who has major potential, believed in them, and who are willing to spend their time and own money to work with us in building a successful music career!

Why Choose Us ?

3 DECADES OF MUSIC BUSINESS EXPERIENCE
Platinium and Gold Records
MOTOWN RECORDS
UNIVERSAL
SONY
CAPITOL RECORDS

WE WORKED WITH:
Kanye West - Jay Z - Stevie Wonder - Michael Jackson - Germaine Jackson - Smokey Robinson - Dionne Warwick - Cheryl Lynn - The Originals -

Digital Marketing Services
SOCIAL MEDIA - STREAMING SERVICES - MUSIC DISTRIBUTION - PRESS RELEASE - PRESS DISTRIBUTION - PR

Radio Airplay and TV Commercial
TERRESTRIAL AND DIGITAL RADIO CAMPAIGN AL GENRES EXCEPT HEAVY METAL - CABLE TV AND MAJOR NETWORK COMMERCIAL

Licensing & Booking
CONCERTS, LIVE MUSIC, EVENTS, CLUB NIGHTS - RED CARPETS - FOREIGN LICENSING AND SUBOPUBLISHING

📞 **1-818-514-0038**
(Ext. 1)
Monday - Friday / 9am to 6pm

FIND US :

www.YourMusicConsultant.com
30721 Russell Ranch Road Suite 140 Westlake Village, USA
Email : info@yourmusicconsultant.com

Christmas Gifts Ideas!

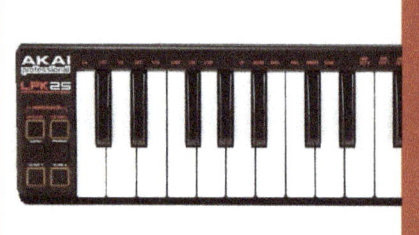

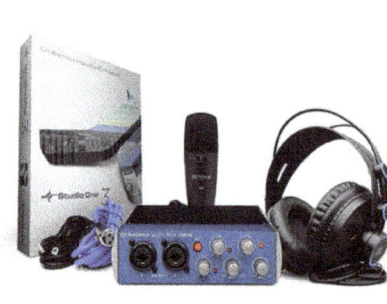
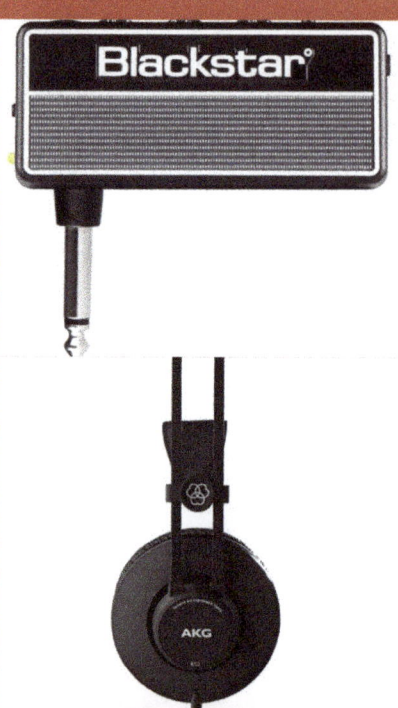

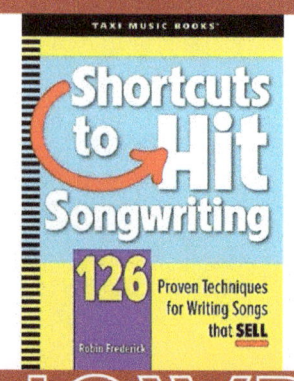

FOR SONGWRITERS & MUSICIANS

Your loved ones deserve a gift just as unique as their passion.

WEST END ORGANIX

Ageless Beauty, Organic Health

BLACK SEED OIL

HEALTHY IMMUNE SYSTEM
INFLAMMATORY RESPONSE

www.westendorganix.com

HOME MADE
BEAUTY TIPS

ESSENTIAL AND NATURAL HOMEMADE BEAUTY TIPS FOR FAIRNESS SKIN THAT PEOPLE SHOULD DEFINITELY TRY OUT AND FOLLOW ON A REGULAR BASIS.

1. AVOCADO AND RICE POWDER MASK:

This is not only a mask but this is also an exfoliator. This is very good for people having dry and sagging surface. People who has dryness and needs Moisturization they can benefit with this. The powder will help to exfoliate and the avocado contains excellent moisturising properties. These can be very helpful.

People can mix about 1 cup of pulp of avocado which should be ripe and to this about half a teaspoon of grained rice powder.
This should be applied normally and then after 20 minutes, this should be washed off by scrubbing in gentle motions.
The mask will soften the surface and then it can be scrubbed easily.
This should be done as per requirement which can be twice a week.

2. LEMON JUICE AND OLIVE OIL MASSAGE FOR FAIRNESS SKIN:

This is very good for those having sagging and old surface. This can be good for those who have clogged pores because warm olive oil will help to open the ores. At the same time, the lemon juice helps to mildly bleach the surface and give a glowing effect.
About 1 teaspoon of good brand olive oil can be taken and slightly warmed up.
To this about 1 teaspoon of fresh lemon juice can be mixed.
Massage on for about 6 minutes and then wash off with a cleanser.
This should only be done a few times a week.
This should be avoided or the lemon juice used in less quantity if these is irritating to the person using this.

BEAUTY

3. TEA BAG SOAK FOR TIRED EYES:

This is a very popular method to soothe the tired eyes. People having dry or dullness around the eyelids, can try soaking tea bags in warm water and then take these to get chilled in the refrigerator.
Then these can be put directly over the area and then the person can lie down for about 15 minutes. This is the treatment time. Then the eyes and also the surrounding area will feel freshen. This can regularly be followed to get rid of any patches or even bags.

4. APPLE AND HONEY PACK FOR FAIRNESS SKIN:

This is a moisturizing and anti oxidant mixture. This can be used even when a person is doing fruit facial. This can be a good thing for a paste that can make a person freshen. This rejuvenated and also makes dull surface to improve the complexion. The honey is also anti bacterial and therefore can be good for those having rashes. It is also good for those who need excessive Moisturization. This can be quite helpful to them.

The apples can be peeled and then grated.
The juice can be squeezed out and then mixed with honey about 2 tablespoons or as per requirement.
This can be applied for about 20 minutes and then washed off.
The antioxidants will get soaked and give freshness.

5. STEAM IT CLEAR:

One of the easiest way to get a clear and fair skin within minutes it to opt for a face sauna where you hover over a warm water bowl possibly with a few drops of essential oil in it as you lock in the area with a overhead towel and allow the steam to make wonders on your face. Steaming is always best beauty tip for fairness skin.

6. SCRUB AWAY FOR FAIRNESS SKIN:

Scrubbing is an integral part of skin lightening where the scrub often made of grainy ingredient helps you relax your skin whilst improving blood circulation while the coarse face pack draws out the underlying dirt and moisture and cleanses and clears up your face. To make a good homemade scrub simply use grained sugar and salt with a tea spoon of yogurt to make a mixture. Massage well before washing off.

7. LEMON HONEY PACK FOR FAIRNESS SKIN:

Lemon is considered a good exfoliator as the citrus in it seeks and clears out the dirt and lightens the skin from the dermal layers. Honey is considered a natural soother that brings a warm glow to your skin. so why not mix these two for good homemade beauty tips for fairness. Squeeze some lime or lemon with some honey and use it as a pack.

Funk Therapy

| Funky | Trendy | Cool | Hip |

Wear The Music You Love!

Visit our merchandise store on our website:

WWW.FUNKTHERAPYMUSIC.COM

10% Discount code: STAYFUNKY

- Hoodies
- Crop Top
- Sweat Pants
- Bucket Hats
- Slides
- Mugs

UNISEX T-SHIRTS

Brown T-Shirt

GRAB IT NOW

Orange T-Shirt

GRAB IT NOW

Beige T-Shirts

GRAB IT NOW

Join our community
@funktherapy2

Wellness

HOW TO SAY NO!
Protecting Yourself and Feeling Confident

Saying 'No' isn't just a refusal; it's a potent tool for maintaining balance, setting boundaries, and safeguarding your mental health. Frequently underestimated, the ability to say 'No' is vital across different life facets, from effectively managing personal time to nurturing healthier relationships. Exploring the significance of saying 'No,' let's delve into ten compelling reasons why mastering this skill matters and discover actionable tips for executing it with effectiveness

I. PRESERVING YOUR TIME AND ENERGY:
Prioritize commitments and assess alignment with your priorities before agreeing. Politely decline by stating, *"I'd love to help, but I'm currently committed elsewhere."*

II. ESTABLISHING BOUNDARIES:
Communicate your limits directly yet respectfully. For instance, *"I appreciate your offer, but I'm unable to take on extra tasks right now."*

III. PROTECTING YOUR MENTAL HEALTH:
Understand that saying "No" isn't selfish; it's a form of self-care. Kindly decline if something doesn't contribute positively to your well-being, saying, *"I need to take care of myself right now."*

IV. EMPOWERING PERSONAL GROWTH:
Evaluate opportunities before committing. Decline distractions to allow experiences fostering personal and professional growth.

V. STRENGTHENING RELATIONSHIPS:
Be honest and gracious in your declines. Express appreciation while declining politely, such as, *"I'm honored, but I'm unable to participate at this time."*

VI. ENHANCING DECISION-MAKING:
Pause before agreeing impulsively. Consider your commitments and use language like, *"Let me check my schedule and get back to you."*

VII. DEVELOPING ASSERTIVENESS:
Practice saying "No" gradually. Use positive language such as, *"I need to focus on my priorities right now."*

VIII. ENCOURAGING SELF-CARE:
Prioritize yourself without guilt. Emphasize the importance of self-care by saying, *"I've scheduled personal time that I can't change."*

IX. LEARNING TO PRIORITIZE:
Recognize your limits and the urgency of requests. Decline politely by stating, *"It doesn't align with my priorities."*

X. SAYING 'NO' WITHIN FAMILY OR PARENTAL CONTEXTS:
Respectfully decline within family or parental contexts, ensuring clear communication and understanding of your boundaries. Express gratitude and understanding while politely declining, such as, *"I appreciate your request, but at the moment, I'm unable to accommodate."*

X!. EFFECTIVE COMMUNICATION:
Use direct yet polite language. Offer a brief explanation if necessary, without over-explaining. Be assertive yet kind: *"I'm sorry, I'm fully booked at the moment"*

For more helpful tips, visit www.pumpitupmagazine.com/wellness

GLOBAL FREQUENCY

**EVERYDAY 5PM (PST)
KPIU RADIO**

LISTEN TO GLOBAL FREQUENCY EVERYDAY

HIP HOP - R&B - EDM

5PM - 6PM (PST) ON WWW.KPIURADIO.COM

**HIP HOP - R&B - EDM
HOSTED BY GRANDMIXER GMS**

kpiuradio.com

**@KPIURADIO
@PUMPITUPMAGAZINE**

**SONG REQUEST
KPIURADIO.COM/DEDICACES-1**

WWW.KPIURADIO.COM

HOW TO HEAL WITH BINAURAL BEATS & SOLFEGGIOS FREQUENCIES

Ancient melodies hold the secrets of well-being, and within Solfeggio Frequencies' harmonies lies transformative healing. Let's explore each note's unique resonance and its contributions to our health.

BINAURAL BEATS:

Alpha Waves 8–12 Hz Relaxation, creativity, stress reduction, calm focus
Beta Waves 14–40 Hz Increased concentration, alertness, enhanced cognitive performance
Theta Waves 4–8 Hz Deep relaxation, meditation, access to the subconscious mind
Delta Waves 0.5–4 Hz Deep sleep, healing, restoration, regeneration

SOLFEGGIOS FREQUENCIES

I. 174 Hz - The Foundation of Healing: Effects on pain relief, tension reduction, stress alleviation, and its connection to physical healing, establishing the groundwork for wellness.

II. 285 HZ - Restoring Energy and Balance: Its influence on tissue healing, immune enhancement, root chakra balance, and its role in restoring emotional equilibrium.

III. 396 HZ - Liberating from Fear and Guilt: This frequency aids in releasing fear-based thinking, transforming grief, and facilitating emotional healing.

IV. 417 HZ - Releasing Negativity and Emotional Healing: Potential to dispel negativity, aid trauma recovery, restore emotional equilibrium, and promote restful sleep.

V. 432 HZ - Resonance with Natural Harmony: Alignment with Earth's frequency, anxiety reduction, DNA repair, and fostering creativity.

VI. 528 HZ - The Love Frequency: Reputation for nurturing love, fostering positivity, DNA repair, and enhancing creative inspiration.

VII. 639 HZ - Harmonizing Relationships: Potential to mend relationships, enhance emotional expression, and foster forgiveness.

VIII. 741 HZ - Expressing Authenticity: Role in detoxification, authentic emotional expression, dispelling lies, and aiding in truth-seeking.

IX. 852 HZ - Awakening Intuition: Impact on intuition, spiritual awareness, and role in self-understanding and personal growth.

X. 963 HZ - Transcending Consciousness: Association with higher consciousness, cosmic connection, and accessing divine knowledge.

Solfeggio Frequencies offer a path to holistic healing. For an enhanced experience, use headphones or earphones while exploring these therapeutic tones on platforms like YouTube or streaming services. Embrace the potential benefits for personal well-being and inner harmony.
Wishing you peace, vitality, and a melody-filled path to holistic health! For more insights, visit www.westendorganix.com and embark on your journey towards inner balance and well-being!

"Crossword puzzles help human brain function."

Many people believe this statement, but can't support it with research and trusted sources; that is, until now! The health benefits of crossword puzzles are not limited to cognitive function, though. Here are the five primary yet surprising health benefits of crossword puzzles.

CROSSWORDS DELAY MEMORY LOSS AND HELP ALLEVIATE DEMENTIA.

When most people ask if crosswords are good for brain health, they're most likely wondering if crosswords help strengthen memory. As this study found, solving crossword puzzles later in life delayed memory decline by 2.5 years in those who had developed dementia. Previous education of the participants was not a factor in the results.

In similar studies, researchers found that these benefits help those who are already at risk for Alzheimer's or dementia the most. In other words, if you're at risk for Alzheimer's or dementia, you may benefit from regularly enjoying crossword puzzles.

CROSSWORDS PRESERVE MEMORY, COGNITIVE FUNCTION, AND OVERALL BRAIN STRENGTH.

In another study, researchers found that those who regularly do crosswords have the brain strength of someone 10 years younger than themselves. Scientists and researchers have also found that solvers will get the most cognitive benefits of crossword puzzles by consistently challenging themselves. You can challenge yourself even more with crosswords by:

Increasing the size and/or difficulty of the puzzle regularly.
Timing yourself as you solve the crossword.
Using fewer materials to help you solve.
Solving foreign language crosswords.

YOU CAN STRENGTHEN YOUR VOCABULARY AND SPELLING THROUGH CROSSWORDS.

Crosswords strengthen the vocabulary and spelling of students and adults alike. A larger vocabulary, in turn, can increase your processing speed and your abstract thinking. This kind of mental boost can lead to greater professional success, as well.

And crosswords don't strengthen vocabulary and spelling alone. Solving crosswords can also boost your knowledge of trivia, which has similar cognitive benefits.

SOLVING CROSSWORDS AS A GROUP STRENGTHENS SOCIAL BONDS.

By solving crosswords with friends and family, you'll strengthen your social bonds through fun and conversation. Social connections help you live longer and improve your quality of life. More importantly, a lack of social connection is a greater detriment to health than issues such as obesity and smoking. In other words, inviting your friends over for a crossword-solving party could have just as much of an impact on your health as exercise.

CROSSWORDS ALLEVIATE ANXIETY, WHICH WILL IMPROVE YOUR MOOD.

There are still ways to achieve emotional health benefits from crosswords as a solo solver. For example, more intellectually stimulating exercises might improve anxiety. A study found that people with anxiety were more successful at tasks requiring concentration – such as crosswords – than activities most people consider more "relaxing." This finding relates to the idea that stress beats anxiety by redirecting nervous energy to a task that requires problem-solving.

Find-a-word
THE HUMAN BODY

H	E	A	R	I	N	R	E	T	A	W
L	H	U	M	A	N	N	I	A	R	B
L	R	E	A	G	M	A	C	B	G	O
E	S	I	A	T	O	L	O	S	H	N
M	E	R	H	R	T	I	N	N	T	E
S	N	E	I	D	T	V	T	E	S	S
S	S	A	N	O	E	E	R	Y	L	E
L	E	A	E	O	R	O	O	E	L	C
L	S	O	S	L	N	T	L	O	E	E
E	O	R	G	B	A	N	S	A	B	R
C	O	U	C	S	E	U	S	S	I	T

Instructions: Find the underlined words in the above find-a-word.

The human body is a complex machine. It is made up of cells, organs and tissues. Around 60% of the body is water. A baby is born with 270 bones, and this decreases to 206 by adulthood. The brain is the control centre and takes in information from the five senses (sight, hearing, smell, taste and touch). The heart pumps blood around the body, keeping it alive.

HOW TO HANDLE THE HATERS!
A Survival Guide in Navigating Criticism

In a world buzzing with opinions and connections, encountering critics and naysayers has become an almost inevitable part of our journey. These individuals, often labeled as "haters," can cast shadows on our path, attempting to sow seeds of doubt and negativity. However, mastering mental strength in the face of such adversity is not only possible but empowering.

EMBRACING THE HATER DYNAMIC
Haters, in their various forms, can emerge due to diverse reasons – jealousy, differing perspectives, or personal biases. Their negativity might stem from their own unresolved issues or insecurities. It's vital to realize that their opinions often say more about them than they do about you.

NAVIGATING HATERS IN THE SOCIAL MEDIA SPHERE

Social media, with its boundless reach and instantaneous interactions, has become a breeding ground for haters seeking to spread negativity. Dealing with haters on these platforms requires a different approach. One effective strategy is to curate your online environment by moderating comments and limiting exposure to toxic interactions. Responding with dignity and grace, or sometimes choosing not to engage at all, can disarm hostility. Furthermore, channeling energy into creating positive, engaging content can shift the focus from negativity to your message. Remember, your online presence is a reflection of your brand; showcasing resilience and positivity amidst adversity can often speak louder than engaging in futile arguments.

STRATEGIES FOR HANDLING HATERS
Maintain Perspective: Recognize that not all criticisms are constructive. Discerning between genuine feedback and baseless negativity is crucial. Embrace valuable insights while disregarding unfounded criticism.

Confidence is Key: Holding onto your self-belief is a powerful defense. Understanding your worth and the value you bring helps build an unshakeable foundation against unwarranted negativity.

Respond with Composure: Reacting impulsively to haters can escalate situations. Instead, respond calmly or not at all. Sometimes, silence speaks louder than words.

Learn and Adapt: Every critique, no matter how harsh, holds a potential lesson. Reflect on criticisms to extract valuable insights that can spur personal growth and improvement.

NURTURING MENTAL FORTITUDE
Dealing with haters necessitates mental resilience and a strong mindset. Surround yourself with a supportive network of friends, mentors, or like-minded individuals who uplift and inspire. Engage in self-care practices such as meditation, exercise, or hobbies to fortify your emotional resilience.

THE EMPOWERING MINDSET
In the grand symphony of life, haters are merely background noise. Their negativity should not dictate your path or hinder your progress. Instead, view their criticisms as opportunities for growth and introspection.
Remember, your journey towards success and self-fulfillment is unique. Haters are mere spectators; their opinions need not hold weight in your narrative.
Mastering mental strength in the face of haters is a testament to your resilience. By discerning between valuable feedback and baseless negativity, nurturing confidence, and fostering emotional resilience, you can defy the critics and continue on your path with determination and fortitude.
Defy the odds. Embrace your journey. Thrive.

WELLNESS

MENTAL DETOX

- Drink More Water
- Take A Relaxing Batch
- Set Goals For The Next Month
- Learn A New Hobby
- Find A New Podcast To Listen To
- Write Out A Bucket List
- Get 8 Hours Of Sleep
- Read A Favorite Book
- Do 30 Minutes Of Yoga

@pumpitupmagazine

The 5-Days Love Yourself Challenge

- **Day 01** — Write Down What You Love About You
- **Day 02** — Create A Happiness Playlist
- **Day 03** — Cook Yourself A Nice Meal
- **Day 04** — Practice Self-Affirmation
- **Day 05** — Approach Your Problem With Mindfulness

@pumpitupmagazine

How anxious are you?

OVER THE LAST 2 WEEKS, HOW OFTEN HAVE YOU BEEN BOTHERED BY THE FOLLOWING PROBLEMS	Not at all	Several days	More than half the days	Nearly every day
Feeling nervous, anxious or on edge	◯ 0	◯ 1	◯ 2	◯ 3
Not being able to stop or control worrying	◯ 0	◯ 1	◯ 2	◯ 3
Worrying too much about different things	◯ 0	◯ 1	◯ 2	◯ 3
Trouble relaxing	◯ 0	◯ 1	◯ 2	◯ 3
Feeling afraid, as if something awful might happen	◯ 0	◯ 1	◯ 2	◯ 3

What your total score means Your total score is a guide to how severe your anxiety disorder may be: •0 to 4 = mild anxiety•5 to 9 = moderate anxiety•10 to 14 = moderately severe anxiety•15 to 21 = severe anxietyIf your score is 10 or higher, or if you feel that anxiety is affecting your daily life, call your doctor

HELPING OTHERS

It is often said that charity begins at home, and helping others is one of the most important ways to make the world a better place. To be able to truly help those in need, we must first recognize that there is a problem. Whether it's poverty, homelessness, or any other social issue, it's crucial to understand the root of the problem before we can move forward and provide assistance. This blog post will discuss the importance of recognizing that there is a problem and why it should be the first step to making a difference.

ACKNOWLEDGING THAT THERE IS A PROBLEM

Making the world a better place can seem like a daunting task. But if we start by recognizing the problems that exist and then take steps to help address them, we can have a real and lasting impact. It all starts with acknowledging that there is a problem.

It's easy to think that our own lives are the only ones that matter, and that problems in other parts of the world don't affect us. But when we come to understand the interconnectedness of our global community, we can recognize the importance of making a difference. We can see how helping others can actually make the world a better place for everyone.

The next step is to figure out how to make a positive impact. This could be as simple as volunteering at a local soup kitchen or donating money to a charity. It could also mean advocating for policy change or lending your voice to an important cause. No matter what you choose to do, it's important to realize that small efforts can have a big effect.

Finally, it's important to stay committed and take action. Every day brings new opportunities to make the world a better place, so look for ways to contribute and do your part. It may not seem like much at first, but if we all work together, we can create real and lasting change.

TAKING ACTION

We all have a part to play in making the world a better place. It begins with recognizing that there is a problem, and then following up with actions that will help make a positive difference. To help us all make a bigger impact, here are some practical ideas on how to make the world a better place:

1. Practice Kindness – A little kindness can go a long way in making the world a better place. Showing compassion, understanding, and empathy can help improve our relationships with others and create a more harmonious atmosphere.

2. Spread Positivity – Instead of engaging in negative conversations, try to focus on being optimistic and uplifting those around you. Encourage others to think positively about the world, and share your own ideas for how we can make it better.

3. Volunteer – If you have the time and resources, volunteering can be a great way to help those in need and make a positive contribution to society. Whether it's helping out at a soup kitchen or helping the elders, providing free services at a music charity event or an animal shelter, there are plenty of ways to get involved.

4. Support Local Causes – Supporting local causes in your area can help make a big difference. Take some time to research local initiatives in your community and see what you can do to get involved.

5. Donate – If you can afford it, donating money to causes that support social justice, environmental conservation, and poverty alleviation can make a huge difference. Even small donations can help provide much-needed funds for those who are struggling.

www.ingramcontent.com/pod-product-compliance
Lightning Source LLC
LaVergne TN
LVHW072251060526
838201LV00070B/4974